ATONEMENT

ATONEMENT

{ *poems* }

Judith Harris

LOUISIANA STATE UNIVERSITY PRESS

baton rouge   MM

For Walter and Alani

With special gratitude to Pati Griffith, Jeff Berman, Don Hall, Michael Harper,
Pam Presser, and Connie Shade.

Manufactured in the United States of America
First printing
09   08   07   06   05   04   03   02   01   00
5   4   3   2   1

Designer: Barbara Neely Bourgoyne
Typeface: Bembo
Printer and binder: Thomson-Shore, Inc.

Library of Congress Cataloging-in-Publication Data

Harris, Judith, 1955–
    Atonement : poems / Judith Harris.
        p. cm.
    ISBN 0-8071-2610-1 (cloth : alk. paper) — ISBN 0-8071-2611-X (pbk. : alk. paper)
    I. Title.

PS3558.A6466 A96 2000
811'.54—dc21

00-040559

The author gratefully acknowledges the editors of the following journals, in which some
of the poems herein first appeared, sometimes in slightly different forms: *Antioch Review,
American Scholar, Boulevard, English Journal, Greensboro Review, Hiram Review, Journal of the
American Medical Association, Midstream, Midwest Quarterly, New York Quarterly, Nimrod, Poet
Lore, Poetry Northwest, Prairie Schooner, Sojourner: The Woman's Forum, South Florida Poetry
Review, Southern Humanities Review, 13th Moon, Webster Review, West Branch, Wisconsin Review,*
and *The Women's Review of Books.*
    "Matrushka Dolls" appeared in *Her Face in the Mirror: Jewish Women on Mothers and
Daughters,* ed. Faye Moskowitz (Beacon, 1994), as well as in the New York *Forward,* Octo-
ber 14, 1994. "Maria" appeared in *Hungry As We Are: An Anthology of Washington Area Poets,*
ed. Ann Darr (Washington Writers Publishing, 1995).

The Earth might in certain ways be alive—not as the ancients saw her . . . —more like a tree. A tree that exists, never moving except to sway in the wind, yet endlessly conversing with the sunlight and the soil.

—James Lovelock

Contents

ATONEMENT

Matrushka Dolls

How many coats of darkness can there be
as the child falls asleep,
like a story within a story;
or a doll within a larger doll
like the wooden dolls
my mother wrapped up in two small boxes
and carried home from Haifa.

Green dresses, bowed kerchiefs,
and painted faces,
bellies halved and shellacked
in bakers' aprons,
girths wide
as the earth itself,
belted with a tiny crack
at the middle.

My mother never told me
how babies were born,
only that the body
unscrewed itself like a jar
and that the shell peeled open;
and inside was the seed that would
begin the child, like a sprout, growing:

a girl within a finished girl
as a maze uncoiled upon the map
or a bobbin of thread unwinding,
or a branch unraveled
from the licorice twist of wind
or the sky lifting up
yet another hollowed mask.

Now I have my own daughter,
a scroll of flaxen hair laid
in the spread palms of afternoon,

and I wonder
what she dreams
as she spirals down
into the dark orchard I meant
to plant inside her
and the darker orchard underneath.

And there a gardener gathers
under the base of each tree
more red and gold in airy baskets,
until, one day, my daughter will eat the flaky seed
that will split her in two
and break the sky
with a cranny of thunder.

My daughter was born in summer
among the lemons and roses.
What my mother told me
whispered again in my ear:
how a child snaps out
from a tree,
and the cored world circles
and circles around
the black mouth of its own equator,
sealing itself back together again.

Through the Window

All day they've been
chopping away at the oak.
Below, in my neighbor's yard,

three struggle against
the stiffened torso,
pitching a rope
to balance their weight
against a sudden fall.

From the nursery window,
I can hear the splitting—
smaller and smaller cuts
tearing at the seams:

the sweet scent
of yellow sap
sieving the air.

When my daughter
goes down for her nap,
I see how sunlight
gluts back in her room,

and the old tree's carping
at the windowlight
is dulled, then quiet. There,
on the grass,

only the scatter
of gold dust,
and men in flannel jackets
rooted as housewives
bowed over their brooms.

I pause at the glass,
looking out at a space
where an invisible outline
is redrawn in the mind,

tucking in branches,
and the minions
of parenthetical leaves.

Such are the things
of this world,
that divide and divide

only to discard themselves
into the one envisaged form,
where the Beautiful
unwillingly disappears.

My Mother Crying While Man
Reaches the Moon, 1969

The shades drawn,
my mother's pool of darkness
private as blood. Cicadas whirr at the windowpane.
Mother in housecoat at five o'clock.

In another part of the house
a flat-footed and blubbery maid
dips chicken wings in a basket. My sister
blows on her flute. I fit gold trees into
the empty links of a puzzle.

Something sends me down
the long, drafty hall, past
the square of a seascape
to the brittle crack of her door,
into the big, forbidden room

where my mother lies on her bed
moaning, her bun unraveled
and touching one shoulder,
mouth wide open—
a semicircle of white teeth
glimmering in a black tunnel.

I have never seen my mother cry.
She has always hidden hurt away
behind a wall
like her nakedness,
or let it fall, drop by drop,
on the spread jackets of an onion;
or gulped it down whole
like a pill in public.

But tonight
she covers nothing, buttons undone,
the thin copper spark of her sex showing.

She cries out of summer,
heat buzzing up from the marshes,
the dry organdy hills,
sugar maple, martins
swooped low in the stalled fits of light;
my father's shoe at the door,
the backyard plastered with yellow flowers.

She cries
while the astronauts lift off at Cape Canaveral
in a twinkle of fire and smoke,
until the moon's lump is cold
and she holds me close, taking my hand
in hers so I can feel the oils of her flesh,
the soft blast of her heart like an engine.

She tells me never to love a man,
he will leave you alone
to walk the light-headed hours.
My mother looks up to the ceiling,
imagining paint speckles as stars.

She says the moon is only a man's target,
a distracted gold trophy,
and she is already far beyond it,
fluttering through daydream,
through the unbearable hoops of female blackness
winding into the howl of unsteady space.

And for the first time
I know that my mother
is a rocket.
In a blue room padded with pillows
she spins out of this world—

to where the sky dares to roll back
its final double seam
as she glides face-up in the air;

until there is nothing
but hollow trembling
and at last the coming of sleep.

Keepsake Drawer

Once opened, it was more than a secret,
a walled-in garden painted with perfume.
The satin purse, and single blue garter,
a matchbook stolen from Gary Cooper's
brownstone parlor, the beret
she wore on Armistice Day, when,
red-lipped, she had to stand on line

with more elegant girls and welcome home
the tired soldiers with a small papery kiss.

Perhaps this was the night she met my father—
at a dance where she wore the strapless dress
pleated like an accordion, black
and powdered with peacocks. At least,
this is how my mother liked to tell it,
with a flair for romance:
the bobbing lanterns whirling
over the silver-bossed dance floor;
the swoon of the orchestra and gold bassoon.

Her ears smelled like gardenias,
the sky was detailed with stars,
the gazebo wreathed with sprays of unblown
roses; and when her cousin introduced her,
she felt what no one else could—

the swell of moonlight,
and the chill under the separate eaves,
pure white and choked with love.

Jacob's Dream

Flocks herd with their young,
buffeted by the long
sticks of rain.
Darkness pauses;
it is the silence before all things.

At least this place was certain.
Baskets of figs,
the moon's soft dial.
Someone takes stones
and sets them for pillows.
You bow yourself seven times before sleep.

The hills are far away.
Women eat raisins and carry their sons.
What are you thinking
so close to the stars?
When the ladder is set
up to the earth—
reaching toward heaven—

the sky appears more fluent
in its radiant shining,
and the bushes
extend their bronzed fruit,
slow emissaries of light; and a name.

Indian Summer at the Estate Sale

We believe in former lives,
some of us.
A warm wind belonging to summer
bends through the thinning trees.

People move through
the open patio, passing
display tables draped with velvet,
glittering pendants,
shocks of crystal gems.

Who can resist thinking
of the others—
their names, by now, have worn
from the bootsoles,
the sewn-in tags.
And who would not care
to imagine them
in these vacant rooms,
dressing before the bay-cold windows,
shrugging off nightgowns,
or spooning marmalade
in the breakfast nook downstairs—
their best things
stowed away in boxes and trunks?

Perhaps they've always whirled abroad
only to return
with a nostalgia for accent,
the striking charm
of weather none could predict.

Along the tour of hallways
and fanning stairs,
they still offer themselves to the touch:

a beaded bag, or baby's jacks,
a black satin bow,
dishes embossed with sylvan flowers.

And there, in the backyard garden,
a woman's suit, well-preserved
vintage '50s, nailed
to the torso of a sycamore—

her perfect figure
swinging in the fortunate air,
the backdrop of sky
a blue estate—
for calling the birds back
or pruning gold leaves;
the small bequests of absent borders.

Two Girls in a Churchyard

In summer, the sky laden with thick foliage,
sunlight burnishing the outer rusks
of reascending roses
as morning glories plait
the circular churchyard.

In search of shade, two parochial schoolgirls
hover under the dogwoods;
their laughter cleaves to the ringing bells

as they lean far back on a bench—
meant for penance,
girls, hot, uniformed
under the sluggard branches—
until talk begins to die.

Then they start to stretch—
laps already filled with eroding
shadows of larch and juniper leaves—
and the cool wind they had wanted

leans invisibly against them,
gently, gently,
breaking their fall.

After Summer Storms

After storms were bad,
he would step outside
to distract himself—
puff of a Havana cigar—
grinding his shoe down
on a jagged rock on the lawn.
I would watch through the window,
waiting for the voices to die out
as my mother climbed
the stepladder,
stacking veined dishes above her head.

And when it was not
too cloudy, my father would
bring down the telescope
in its black-and-gold box,
and set up the tripod
on the porch's asphalt steps.
He'd crouch
as big men do, when forced—
steering the wild backdrop of sky
into focus while the moon
squinted like a gem.
Above, the birch trees' gossip
songbirds slapped hard wings
at the pulled-in stars.

What was he aiming for?
Among the tiny lassoes of smoke rings,
and coins tinkling low in his pockets,
he was always looking for
the face of the satyr,
or a damaged piece of lunar matter;
and when he couldn't find it,
he would stagger back to the house
like a hunter

lugging his junked traps,
the long tubes of the lenses,
unscrewed, uncuffed,
laid back like silver flutes
from shortest to long
in their red velvet beds.

This is what I knew of space
and my father's temper:
the spinning of the planets,
Saturn's rings like a pinwheel
of circus colors, and Pluto always farthest—
a cold and tempting plum.
But I did not know what he saw
those nights,
banking on some sign to appear
saintly or monstrous,
peeking with one eye closed—

while I asked for forgiveness,
seeing God like my own father,
middle-aged and adrift
in the motionless garden:
one who cranks this world
so slowly that nothing is felt—
and I would think of the hands,
how they, too, must be wide open
and stinging
from bringing so much anger
into unspeakable love
like the flashing beauty of thunder
that leaves no mark.

Silver's Beauty Parlor

Through a silver mirror glass,
my mother has learned to disappear,
while I flip through *Glamour* and *Redbook*
and pretend to be adult
under the whirl of the dryer:
its steel drum pressed tight around my ears,
the inside of a giant egg,
burning summery air.

The shampoo girl
leads her to the sink,
where she rubs and cradles
my mother's puttied head
until it bubbles like a sparkling tiara.
She pours the winking bottle of yellow dye
that will turn her chestnut hair
from dark to light.

Wisps of scattered curls
keep falling gray and brown
as the clap of scissors
flutters round and round, a wand!

Brushed and teased, sprayed with
puffs of purple lilacs, she takes my sleeve
and we swing out the jingling door
as she counts out our taxi change.
Magically, she has become
the blonde she says she was
when she was my age.

It is already twilight,
the shop brings down its slatted shades,
the bald man owner comes out
to fold the Zorro capes, and smooths
tomorrow's wrinkled bills.

Meanwhile, the wigged mannequins
keep careful watch
like faceless crystal balls:
Honey-Sun, or Halo,
Midnight, Ash, and streaks of Dawn.

Accident

Too warm for a coat,
I pass shrunken snowmen
on the spotted yards of Applewood Street—
an hour past my music lesson.

Carrying the case home like an armor,
the violin sleeping
in a red velvet bed,
I am still climbing the scale
like a stair in my head,
I am still daubing the string.

Failure again.
I can't reach the high note,
and I think of the highest things I know:
the sky and its dark frosting;
the night pricked with tiny wind holes.
Above, the dead live,

as we do, but know more.
At the corner, I am watching the sky,
not the ground,
imagining beautiful sonatas
passed down from it
to the flutish birds,

and when the car comes,
I am not looking,
I am not looking.

It is hard coming back to earth
where gravity kisses our soles.
Later, they tell me I am lucky—

my instrument is broken
instead of my bones, and the horsehair

bow has frayed it's smooth mane.
They give me paper slippers to wear.
My real shoes stuck like blue eggs
in the thistles of a tree.

When they ask me
what I was doing, I tell them
I was looking up in the air,
and then I was struck,

flying over the top of my town,
over the clanging bells
and airplane sputters.

I do not tell them
that when it happened,
I was only talking to God.

The Tea Party

From Mother's costly Wedgwood,
we set out teacups
on the resting lawn;
the sun stood over us,
chiming like a servant's bell.

We offered our guests
lemons, wafers—
my sister in feather cap
and ropes of pearls.
I followed orders,
played the spinster maid,
as she opened that weighty book
of Manners,
instructing me
on where to place
the proper spoon and plate.

Where was Mother?
Lying down in her bed,
or adding up figures
from a cigar box clumped with bills—
while we took turns
being Queen under the hunchback oak,
sailing to China
along the equator's gold hem;
leaving her alone to pace
among the Florentine chairs
and tabletops,
minutes rolling off the shuddering clock
until Father would return.

Poor Mother, sick these long days,
would have died to see
her treasures
purloined

from the claw-legged serviere,
and nearly toppled
in a heap of potted loam.

It was a miracle nothing broke—
as we curtsied round the garden vines,
spinning out our own Odyssey
like braids of bundled yarn.
We asked, "Who should we
invite in twenty years?"
while looking into the half-spheres
of maiden cups,

while inside the west-end window
Mother sewed
and sipped the light in wistful,
doled-out drops. . . .

The Babysitter

She came from a smaller house
down the hill, where the trees were thick
and the creek deep and forbidden.
Hair, honey-blond
and teased in a beehive,
wrists sparkling with the scent
of "Jungle Gardenia,"
she was aspiring to become an actress.
And after feeding us, the goldfish,
and then the parakeet, she would stand at the top
of the stairs to make her grand entrance,
slowly descending,
singing in a husky voice:
"Let me entertain you, let me make you smile . . ."
with a bump and a grind of her hips
just like Gypsy Rose Lee.

Tanned legs swinging from the couch,
my sister and I would clap hands
to the beat of her struts,
stunned by the gradual revelation
as one by one, her clothes
shimmered to the floor:
the white blouse with the little fringe collar,
pleated skirt, bobby socks, half-slip
inching up to her nose like an Arabian veil,
Maidenform bra and cotton panties
trailing piece by piece
until she stood stark naked
on my parents' polite and frozen living-room carpet—
her fake butterfly shyness
shedding its drab cocoon.

All summer, we wouldn't tell.
Soon the whole neighborhood
crowded our house after school.

I remember how we thrilled each time
as her long legs sashayed around the room,
her blouse drooped, and then
the toss of an evening glove
borrowed from Mother—the glimpse
of hard white breasts, or sunburned stomach,
a dross of auburn hair
blurting from her thighs—

and how years later
in the slow summer fanning on the porch
my sister and I
swayed to the waffled tunes
on the upstairs radio,
mimicking her
as she perched on a tabletop—
"I want to be Johnny's Girl"
and "It's Judy's time to cry . . ."

taking our turns, stripping for bed,
teasing off undershirts,
hugging chests bare,
rehearsing for our own lives,
amazed and terrified by
what we might become.

When my father is told

When my father is told
he has cancer,
he takes the wide brown envelope
to the specialist's office,
where each chair is taken,
so he has to keep standing
holding the report,
a schoolboy's failing grades.
Inside, the odd pies of percent,
the fuzzy X ray that shows
where, and how much
had wormed into the pelvic bone,
dark spot the size
of a poker chip.
The doctor rubs his eyes
under his bifocals,
arranging his Byzantine desk
with its sharpened pencils,
paper weight in the block
of a Grecian's golden head.
On his little pad, he scribbles
treatments like homework:
four pills a day,
injections of a female hormone
to starve the testosterone—
and now my big-boned father,
refugee, soldier, union president,
is beaten like a woman,
fearing he'll wake one day,
soft, bare, and singing
as a soprano.
I remember years ago
the August thunder,
my father's heavy foot
shaking the thin floor
as the winds belted the glass,

leaves sticking like
gold ovaries on the pane,
and my father's imitation
of Robert Goulet
from Radio City's *Camelot:*
"If ever I would leave you,
it wouldn't be in summer, oh no . . ."
the lightning cracking,
then the sky, like a plate,
while darkness crossed over,
with all the stars shattering
like crystal,
and my father's brave
Jewish Launcelot
on his knees with arms outstretched . . .
pleading to stay.

Waiting

When you tell me you are dying
I think of early spring, when the dogwoods
are shawls of draining snow,
and I see them pressing,
swaying like the white beards of rabbis
waiting for the Messiah to come.

Then summer passes, stripping off
the spotted leaves, leaving the branches lit
and bare, and still He does not come.

And then the fall, when the cool air
gathers all its stars in our yard
and the glazed cherry
hangs like a child's fist
pounding the hard chest of the sky.

The Model

Each evening she goes to the sitting.
She can barely hear the grackles in the park,
the crossing guard's low whistle.

It is becoming twilight,
the neighborhood stews are warming;
the moon, a comma, swirls above dogwood.

This is the hour when
the little gold keys
pirouette at front doors,
when wives, the color of milk,
press close to the windows.

Although it is fall,
she wears the same summer dress,
revolving in lemons. With a blue thumb,
the wind reels in its leaves.

She thinks this is what it must be like
to be motionless as a stopped clock, or a clinched fly,
or the page-boy manikin in the tailor's shop,

to be, not a body, but a statue.
Now, as night leans to kiss the frail lips
of the moon, someone tells her to hold still,

and she thinks this is the *un*real,
the painted sky and black trees
stretching above the frosted clouds of her town—

and the lungs of flowers, *dark flowers,*
breathing so softly, so perfectly,
no one can see.

Remembering Odessa

Father knew six languages
and sold sewing machines in Odessa.
Before I was a schoolgirl,
I could read in three.
I remember the yellow hair
of my mother, which matched
the wands of wheat in picture books.

They buried her
among a few twisted shrags in the onions
where they had pulled up roots
and dug and dug;

poor mother was too big
for the box, so they had to bend
her knees to fit her in.
The fields were ice, and among the mills,
Polish women were picking mushrooms
off the truck in aproned coats
and blue babushkas.

Men covered my mother
in snow—letting it crack against
the pine lid in all sorts
of lovely, unpredictable ways,
like a foreign alphabet.

I am so old now
my mother seems like my own child.
I can lift her easily,
as the Yiddish sky
boosting the birds and almond trees.

Thinking back, I'm glad
they dressed her in warm boots

borrowed from a sister.
White flakes will be falling
where she is traveling at last,
or else, it could be bare.

Blessing

One for the mother
sifting in lamplight,
her thick dough hand pulling
the ivory tip of a needle;

and for the father
aiming his telescope at the rings
of Uranus,
and for the sister already bumping
her way into stars.

Those nights blessings came to
the glamorous moon,
to the woven limbs of the tree
and its meandering petals;
and then to the smallest nouns
in their invisible sky boxes

before turning again to the dead
for whom blessing meant
counting over again—
filling in the old people's eyes
with joy—their only weather—

this, of course, is just how the dead
choose to leave us alone
in our moveable world:

with a concern, and a silence.
Each night they bless our stones, our grass,
and even more faintly our dust,
one after the other,
but saving our darkness for last.

I Wanted to Be Ivy

Ivy, even the wildflowers stood at attention
at your door. You were
the only one in third grade
who colored straight with a ruler,
up and down, up and down.

I could not understand
your paper world of faint, orderly houses
all trimmed in yellows and pinks,
the chimneys always neat as hatboxes
with a perfect curlicue of smoke.

I wanted to be you, to dazzle all
who swished down those aisles,
so I tried to loosen my hold,

learning to keep
within those boldfaced lines
and not to scribble,
to pour my shape like flesh
inside an hourglass girdle.
Soon, my tulips grew as yours did
in militant rows,
my sharp grass singular as dresspins.

Perfectly now, I crayoned
the framed sky,
the sun rimmed and armed, a clock,

before filling in
the trees' button-round apples.

I was Eve
suddenly arriving
in an immaculate garden.
A horizon behind me,

and green always beneath my feet.
But the birds, poor little hammers,
magenta and yellow
chiding more light to break in.

Violin Lesson

Each Wednesday, I walked it to school
in the blue-shaped hollowness
of morning sky. Blackbirds.
I was their caretaker.
Each one hinged on telephone wire
as if perched on a music page.

Practice was at five P.M.
Taking the rosined bow from its velvet case,
I held cleft to chin,
elbow plowed in a right angle,
as wings screeched up
the wooden scale,
each one a little higher,
the last one on icy E.

Outside, the "Quiet" sign
hung in lopsided tedium
while Mr. Mann, the music teacher,
slumped drunk in his swivel chair.
I had no pitch, no ear,
and quit before the hour ticked down
on the marching metronome,

tiptoed out the gravel road,
only to hear
within the forest's scrolls
the riotous chords of real blackbirds
seating themselves in tuxedoed orchestra,
tuning up in wind and brass—
plucking the strings.

Breach

The tree outside my window
was planted the day I was born.
In spring, its skeins curled taut
on the branches,
purple and white;
its fruit I was warned
might be poisonous.
I came to regard its depth:
leaden in the reared months
of winter;
shade pinned-in
as a crippled wing.
At age ten, comparing my height
to its own tartared crown,
I note the inch, or three,
grown over me.
I never asked its proper name,
whether it was ash, or lilac;
or why my mother planted
on the day of her terrible labor.
I was born upside down,
leaning far back on a swing.
Perhaps there will always be
another sky,
another world, inverted,
another language,
however beautiful, for pain.

After Harsh Words with My Daughter

Last night, the wind banged
against the house
and I woke contrite about being harsh

and entered the pinkish glow
of her nightlit room
to lie down beside her.

And when the dawn broke,
I was still watching the snow
crisscrossing the air,
braying and twining

as the taking and giving
of each of her breaths.
And I thought, what use are words,

sprinkled here or there,
in anger or in love,
as they lie like heeded flecks of snow
that will not stick
upon this sleeping earth?

Jewish Holidays

When I was growing up,
the holy days meant
relighting the Yizkor cups
for the dead, buying a plaid
skirt at Hecht's, on sale,
wearing nylons
and alligator garters
with black pumps.

Shuffling from morning to noon,
I watched the line of
covered bald men
finger their shawls
in wooly auditorium chairs,
opening their prayer books
from right to left,

davening or rocking on rubber soles.
Light streamed through the stained glass,
over a checkerboard
of pillbox hats and yarmulkes,
black, red, and gold
all nodding, amen.

By midday, the wine goblet was set out
in the reception room,
with tiny plastic glasses.
With the last psalm,
we rose and bowed our heads
as they took out the torah
from its draped velour ark,
shaped like an "m"
in two papyrus tablets,
cradled in the usher's arms:

yellow tasseled jacket,
swiveled scroll handles,
held over the shoulders
of the chanting,
like a hero or movie idol—
worshipers kissing
their own hands

and then its cold shoulder;
and there we were,
congregation of Adais Israel,
parted and flowing
through two paths up the aisle,
the coming and the going,
waiting for God's judgment
from the birth of the round world
to the day of atonement,

a mere matter of a week,
as long as cut roses live,
before God with his prophets
decided who would be rich or poor
or who would be saved:
and I looked at my father
crying over a candle for his dead father,
listening for God's voice
like the softest rain
falling through the cedar walls.

My Father's Voice

When you die,
promise you'll come back
and tell me something.
But how will I know it's you?

Will your voice be loud,
be suddenly light
as a girl's in a choir?

I will listen for you,
in the stippling of feathers,
in the caw's syntax,
unique as a thumbprint.

Father, fly now
in your spidery bones,
galled, bejeweled—
an invisible staircase
of colorless leaves—
give me a sign
of what is better than life:

with nothing
but a tree, or a stone,
or the smears of my small hands
at the window glass,

watching for you
in all the darkness to come.

Request

Near the end,
when he thought of the grave,
Keats said he could feel
the daisies growing over him—

daisies, not the violets
he favored, not even the white
carnelian
she'd sent as a gift;

but simple English flowers
rising over the silt,
a helm of yellow suns, abiding
where his heart once was.

This would be his wish:
to be buried with her letters
and a lock of her russet hair;

then to sink, as all bodies do,
to the deepest roots
of love.

Sunset over the Houses Will
Border This Field

The clouds sweep westerly,
carrying their muscle
of sun. Inside the wood,

doorways are endless.
The gold leaves nap on their hinges;
an apron of wildflowers
swells on the hill.

As you go, think back
to all that has happened:
rain, and the burrowing deeper
of stones, the half-moon
set on its tracks and spilling
its gleaned apples,

never to be filled.
And even now,
while the women are laying out
the puffs of white bread on the table,
in rooms ornamented
with butterflies and a corner piano,

they say: come back, little one,
to the night that shines
through their windows.
Soon the elders will flutter;
the days will grow shorter

and the sky, the sky
with an hour's blue knitting
still left to do.

My Husband Dreaming

My husband is dreaming again.
He wants to turn the roof of our house
into a garden.
He has always taken a garden
seriously—and counts on
small and potted cabbage plants
to endure the winds;
and in summer, the close thorns of the sun.

He has all this in mind:
a gazebo to shade the baby,
daffodils, mums, and irises
flourishing above
in the airy dome of his own private kingdom
under the stars.

Above, my husband is already taking
the tools: spade and wimble—
mulch, hoe, and turquoise watering can.
He won't be talked out of it,
although we have no way to get up,
no ladder, or lift, or stairs.

Perhaps he knows better
what is sturdy and clean. After all,
he is the dreamer, and I've learned
not to argue.
One day we will wake
to that garden, moonlit and gasping
at the level of clouds—
like the first couple
staking a lot for creation
and calling it paradise;
knowing no better place
for couples
to set down roots, rise, and then fall.

The Male's Body as Muse

My husband dips into sleep,
his body disguised
by the moon's intrusion.
Astonishingly, he seems still
to be a stranger,
a gathered map
for language.

Only now, the impossible may happen:
my husband can become immortal,
his muscles, taut, smoothed;
his face made young again.

Outside, the trees twist in grievous poses
like the Trojan women
mourning their husbands' bodies
scattered in a pile.
It is a moment of perfect illusion—

men lost inside the siege
of a fatal city;
their outraged bones
finally saved from the dogs, restored.
The widows' wishes
are granted, and they return
with the corpses intact,
no longer begging.

I am not so faithful,
for in the deepest hungers
I hear only a woman's voice
capable of an ancient betrayal—

my husband, the archetype,
sleeps and grows more beautiful, because
I have willed it this way.

Maria

When the small sun yawns,
and creeps back in the maples,
I will tell you the story
of my own Nicaragua,
when I sat, rocking,
in the wobbled light
of one kitchen candle—
then two, in cruddy boots and uniform,
smashed in the door,
scattering duck feathers
where I was mending a pillow.
My hands were tied,
buttons sliced from my dress,
my breasts shivering,
and all the while I could not tell
because the curved moon held
like the policeman's machete
because only the woman knows
how to clench her teeth
and bay like a wolf.
My husband, knee deep
whacking sugar canes in the field,
bundling them back
in the truck,
how could he know
what was happening on the porch
before the shot rang out
as I reeled and fell back
to the earth,
tasting its grit, its salt:
because now it was flesh
because he didn't ask for mercy
because it was his hunger,
moaning my name,
in God's hollow breath,
moaning the way he would

when he lay on top of me,
stinking of tobacco,
wrists nailed to my wrists,
lips to my lips,
tongue to tongue,
this is my story,
the last words
sweating through darkness:
whispering Maria, Maria,
bush of my blood,
here is another fruit of my cock,
another paradise, fluttering in.

Group, Tuesday, Five P.M.

The new girl
speaks low with the grace
of a whisper at church.
Behind her glasses, morning smoke.

The night before
she swallowed two bottles of NyQuil,
a fist of Xanax.
She talks through glass doors, elevators,
the company lawyers, the editor

slashing the veins of her story
in red ink,
she is a ventriloquist,
a phone humming alone on its hook.

I am already her ghost,
her sleeveless billow, an aerosol of posies
in the severed head of the moon
as I slip perfectly
as fingers in a glove

into the tiny apartment
of cut loose-leaf
and stockings draped like nooses
over the shower hose;
the window overlooking the toupees
of black trees, the lizardy bone

of the sidewalk.
Alone, I undo the honey-blonde
haze of her hair,
turning the TV on low,
I am her, whirling like a delicate
wash load in the rotary drum of her pulse.

There is nothing to do but defer, to exist,
a yeasty marvel,
a mad Houdini rising
out of the pool like the prick

of a shark's nose,
through sunken locks, chains, and bubbles.
I am her feet padding to the closet,
her hands fumbling through underclothes,
picking up the vial

with its little bandage
of name and dose,
holding it up to the light

like a tiny wafer,
a wish atoned for in a box,
a velvet flap of purple,
waiting for darkness to open its hatch

from a silver bullet—
an airplane full of sinners
asking to jump;
her shining parachute
with all the colors of the rainbow,

waiting for the earth, then the heavens,
to kiss us good-bye
then let go.

Horseback Riding Lesson

They say it's a girl's first affair,
mastery of the brute,
you carry your velvet helmet,
the leather crop, sugar cubes in a pocket.
Soon you'll have them eating from your hand.

Today's lesson is posting.
Each horse washed and brushed—
by the owner's sons, surname Butts,
bowlegged and sunburned—
Piney, Lucy, Frisky, and Chap;
yours is the slow and more experienced one
led out with a lenient look,
a hobble in his old gait.

You throw on the blanket, then saddle,
buckle the girth, lower the stirrup,
your small grip tight on his mane,
heels digging down in position,
thighs hugging in, slackened reins.
You are in place. You smile like a girl on vacation.

Say you want the horse to know who's boss,
because big as they are, they're just as dumb.
Each Butt broke one in.
That's the secret of training—
you can kick and tug
if your straddle is right—dance on the bone
by keeping him between your baby-fat thighs.

Steered by a nudge, bowing his head,
he teaches you instincts, how to dodge
the slide of the woods, to navigate between
dangling branches of the oak,
and make of yourself a burden that's light.

Preparing My Dress for School

Each night my mother would turn
the dress inside out—pressing its stale flowers
by the sleeves,
inspecting button slits
and puckered waistband
for rips or thinning seams.

Pinning it up
on sharp wire shoulders,
folding down the
spinster collar,
hooking the neck,
letting it hang again,
like the next calendar day,

flat as cardboard,
ruffles layered like a frosted cake.

Snagged ends coy as doll lashes,
my own headless martyr
swung from the peg, all night—
waiting to swallow me whole,
then rise and walk again.

The Wedding Gown My Mother Never Wore

On the chair
in seamed stockings and girdle,
you are surrounded by snips
and measures,
Mrs. Solinsky's new Singer
buzzing
in the attic heat,
pricking you with pins—
hips, bust, and waistline,
the window glass
wiped clean so you could see—

the dress in the making:
darted, basted, and pointed
clockwise to the sun,
your mother spinning you
around like a game of blindman's bluff.

Patience is everything. What a lifetime
it takes to wear just once.
Ask the ivory moon,
the egg shells, sweet flesh of an apple,
leaves hooked to a tree,
everything must go through a fitting.

But today, news will come
of his death over Normandy.
You'll order the dress undone,
plucked of its pearls,
lace untacked, hem unturned . . .
left over bolt of satin laid out for a bedspread,
or buried away in the trunk
along with old army snapshots
of barechested boys stationed in Germany
and the white satin garter
to yellow with age.

Insulin Shot

What did I know then,
watching Grandma shiver,
beet-faced, in the kitchen

over a sink of smogged glasses
and knives,
Grandpa rolling his sleeve up,
making a fist
as if he were going to box?

Blood runs in trees
like so many rivers.
It is blue under the skin.
I see how he winces
at the sight of the needle

as she, dour as any doctor,
jabs it into his arm. . . .
It is 1963,
the sky is slow motion with clouds
while I pivot in the threshold,
holding my breath.

Does it hurt like a bee sting
or the prick of a pin?
I remember the story of William Tell,
and the aim of the arrow.

It is the child in me
that refuses to look.

Atonement

Today, the last chance for amends,
reparations,
the daystar ripens in the den
of moss-colored leaves.

Under a clear sky,
I walk to the market,
vendors offer
their radiant apples, and pears
in straw baskets,

people rummage for ones
unblemished, unbruised.

I want to keep it simple.
I want to ask God to forgive me.

When I die, I want
to walk out of my body, whole,
the way someone walks out of a house
on an ordinary errand.

I want to pick up
this one gold-armored apple
drenched by the dirt and dew,

not out of hunger, but love—
I want to taste
its thronged branches

deep in the rough tears
of its fruit.

Parting My Daughter's Hair

Love, you have inherited my hair,
the static blond fizz, stubborn as weeds,
honey-cooling-in-tea—hair

a cloud drifting over hydrangea,
the crackling aftermath of a storm,
dandelion head,

and I remember,
years past in the woods,
the age you are,
peering out of my second-story window,
spanning the elms
with their crinkled armors,

shrubbery and vines
levitating themselves above
a disorderly garden.

Then, my father,
wielding the rust-covered rake,
parting the white scalp of the earth,

you were my fruit, then,
my glorious child,
wild tresses, unborn,

deep as the root,
and just as ungoverned.

At the Consignment Shop

A man comes in,
rattling the door chimes.
I am in the back,
sorting through designers' clothes,
smelling the cedar wrap and mothballs,
the chill of ancient smoke.

He wants to know if they sell ladies' slips,
half-slips or full.
The woman behind the register
looks at him through a classic
tweed, holding it up for flaws.
She says, "What kind of slip?
Satin or polyester?"

He says he's looking for a cheap one;
already worn.
He offers, "It's for my mother,
to bury her in."

Maybe he wants to dress her properly.
Maybe in life, poor soul,
she was unladylike,
let her ghostly legs shine through.

"But you don't want some outgrown thing,"
the owner quips,
and sends him down the street
to a lingerie shop
where everything from tip to toe
is sold brand new.

Fishing

The summer I turned twelve,
my father taught me
to fish on the lake,
taught me to bait worms on the line,
each tied to a different weight,
a silver magnet.

When the bite came,
he made me yank
and reel back so fast
I tore my sleeve,
and my thumb whip-burned.

That fish fought so hard
I swore it would drag me in,
while my father
kept cussing at me to bring it in,
kicking his foot at the boat.
He wanted that fish the way
some want to win
lotteries, women,
or trophies.

Suddenly, I spun
and ripped out the hook
and threw the fish back,
more out of spite,
into the mouth
of an angry God.

Open House

She marches me in,
among the wooden chairs and books,
and sideboard displays of rocks
and leaves, and butterfly drawings.
"Guess which ones are mine?" she asks,
and I am lost among the stations of the clock,

a colorful array
of swirls, and quilted rainbows,
looking for the one that is marked by
her left-handed scrawl,
a dead giveaway.
Meanwhile, the children
have gathered in the all-purpose room
like a mosaic of pebbles,

some drinking punch in Dixie cups,
or peeking in dioramas.
She tugs at my hand,
pointing out three startled leaves
on her plant on the sill,
before guiding me down
the stairs she's already ascended
like a high note on the scales,

into the music area,
where there is a tuxedo piano
with so many teeth.
And she shows me how
to position my fingers at the keys,
like a reader of Braille,
saying, *"This is like you do*
when you are typing your poems,"

and then she plays a little song,
Beethoven's "Ode to Joy,"

Ninth Symphony, C Major,
while I look out through the steel bars
of the playground,
to the tiny magnifier lens of the moon,

feeling a little helpless, a little small
like lowercase to capital letter,
but suddenly inspired,
asking her to keep place as muse
and teach me, her mother,
how to lift the measured air
of wing and solid bone.

Narcissus

As if I hadn't already dreamt it
a thousand times,
the moment your hand reaches out

to mine,
as a face grazing its own Otherness
in a mirror,
there is no real touch,
no feeling, but the icy numbness of snow
against window glass,

no awakening
but to the sudden tears of thaw.

Fisherman's Flies

Tinsel wings
snipped out of horsehair,
head concealed in its helmet,
emerald thorax,
the compound eye,
exquisite in its glass bier,
all luminous nymphs, or naiads,
hatched not from
larvae but a thin filament's drop
at the stream.
They are beautiful, I say,
not knowing the real from the fake,
from buglike nymph stage to dun,
rainbow to spinners,
all names that ring like a bell:
brown drake, blue-winged olive:
yellow miller, black ghost,
coachman, and mayflies,
eggs reborn, bursting, dodging
like microscopic miniatures
of man's first flying machines,
pinions flapping on arm,
sailing up over the treetops,
foredoomed as winter's only
lightning bug,
flecks of snow hitting
the pond's surface,
then ebbing one by one.
What counterfeit jewels:
a little tarnished
from the wear and tear,
now housed in a tin box,
like sampled candies,
feigning sleep as frozen statues do,
nestled in the sham stillness
of the summer heat,

just catching the rust of sunlight
on the brittle hinges of
their spidery legs
and paintbrush tails.
I think of them all as
sudden masterpieces—
and seem to nudge them irresistably,
as if to shock them
from the airy airlessness
of some human dream,
as if they were not so frail,
or waterlogged,
from all that molting, colliding,
and diving,
only to rise again each time from the dead.

Elegy in Winter Thaw

Today, in the bright January
thaw, under the shirred
brambles of overhung maple,

a few crepe-paper leaves,
I think of you,
fidgety, dark bird,
careening
in the blue lungs of air,

your bodiless laughter
flowing like wood sap
through the grimacing hug

of the branch,
the sky, turned sweet as a river,
and deliberately warming.

Once, it was ice.

After Lacan

One elm
in my neighbor's backyard
shudders in the darkness,

its branches adamant,
still gold.
I have seen it harden
against the cold,

heard its voice
endure,
like an open wound.

And tonight,
somewhere between knowing
and not knowing,
I watch as one by one

its rough leaves,
light downy tufts
in the vein axils beneath,

flicker and blow out,

because of the stars,
because of the inevitable body,

because there are always more
consoling words to fall into,

before us, and after us,
but never our own.

Vocabulary

On the blue back chair, *A World Book* flaps open
its leather wings to kingdoms divided:

moose, water beetle, polar bear, and chameleon:
animals who live in deserts, or jungles;

foxglove, and clumps of grapes or tomatoes:
plants that grow in the woods;

father, son, wife, daughter:
people who live in rooms and sleep in the air;

swallow, finch, bluejay, robin:
birds who paddle the sky during seasons.

This is the earth that began with one word
and all the words that began with a letter,

and all the starry letters in worlds of their own.